CHAPTERS

1. The Beginning   4

2. Settlers Arrive   8

3. The Honeymoon Mecca   12

4. The Daredevils   16

5. The Maid of the Mist   22

6. Niagara's Towers   28

7. The Power of Niagara   30

8. The Tourist   34

9. The Parks   42

10. The Miracles at Niagara   48

11. Niagara in Winter   52

12. The Lights of Niagara   58

13. Niagara Falls, Canada Today   62

14. Facts and Figures   65

Photograph *Entrance to Queen Victoria Park, cicrca 1917. Photo by F.H. Leslie.*

4

Geologists estimate Niagara's roar was first heard on this earth some 12,000 years ago. It began on the edge of the Niagara Escarpment between Queenston on the Canadian side and Lewiston on the American side of the Niagara River. The Falls originated here as continental glaciers receding from the Niagara Escarpment began to creep towards its present location.

Today, like a winding snake, the Falls has gracefully made its way 11 km (7 mi.) from its original beginnings. Along the way, it carved out a spectacular gorge that often takes second billing to the Falls. Now, water diverted for hydroelectric plants has reduced the recession of the Falls to approximately 36 cm. (1 ft.) every ten years.

Over 10,000 years would pass before the Falls would be observed and written about in any detail.

French explorer Samuel de Champlain, a geographer to Henry IV, King of France, first explored Lake Ontario in the early 1600s. While away, he first heard of Niagara Falls. There is neither a record of his trip, nor proof that he ever actually visited Niagara Falls.

Perhaps it was de Champlain's first visit that enticed Robert Cavelier, Sieur de la Salle, to explore Ontario in 1678. La Salle sent an advance party of his expedition to explore the Niagara River. The Recollect priest Father Louis Hennepin, a member of this party, was the first European to write about the Falls.

Although Father Hennepin said the Falls were more than 152 m (500 feet) high, the height of the Falls actually ranged from 52 to 58 m (172 to 190 feet).

La Salle, the leader of the expedition, arrived in Niagara shortly after Hennepin. He soon set about building a small fort on the American side of the border where the Niagara River exits into Lake Ontario. He continued to explore other parts of North America until 1687 when he was murdered by members of his own party. However, credit for establishing the Niagara area as a "new frontier" is given to this French explorer.

Other explorers, both French and British would find their way to Niagara in the next 100 years.

The Original Inhabitants
The first recorded inhabitants of the Niagara Peninsula migrated from the vicinity of London, Ontario around 1300 A.D. Archaeologists have since uncovered sites which are typical of longhouses occupied by tribes of the Iroquoian culture.

When the first Europeans penetrated Niagara, the Iroquoian tribes, consisting of the Senecas, Mohawks, Onondagas, Cayugas and Oneidas were well established and politically organized. Apart from this tribe were the Neutrals and the enemy Hurons. It is believed the Neutrals were at peace with both these tribes and a Neutral village was considered a common "safe" place in the event of war. In fact, the Neutrals inspired the word Niagara.

Not much is known about the Neutrals. French explorers described them as tall and fierce warriors as well as good farmers, fishermen, hunters and excellent traders.

The League of Five Nations (Iroquoian tribes) were highly domesticated.

Men were responsible for defence, land clearing, house building and hunting, while women planted and gathered crops in addition to other domestic duties. Almost everything in an Iroquois village was communal property. This league of nations had an advanced political structure. So successful was their political organization, it would be later cited as a model for the first constitution of the United States.

The arrival of Europeans in the early 1600s began the demise of these proud tribes. Gradually, the Europeans appropriated all of the natives' property and destroyed their proud heritage.

Photographs
Painting (below) by James B. Cockburn, 1833. Young native faces from the turn of the century (left and far right). Acc. 6440 S11705 and S860, Archives of Ontario. Father Louis Hennepin (page 7) was part of the advance party sent by Robert Cavelier, Sieur de la Salle to explore the area in 1678. He was the first European to write about Niagara Falls.

Niagara was originally spelled Onguiaahra. It is popularly believed to be the last surviving word from the language of the Neutral Indians who vanished from this area in the mid 1600s. It first appeared on early French maps as early as 1641. Today's spelling of Niagara is believed to be the written English word for this native spelling. There are two accepted meanings for the word Niagara; "the straight" and "thundering waters." Both translations would have been acceptable, as they are today, to describe Niagara.

On the 6th of December, 1678, St. Nicholas day, we entered the beautiful river Niagara, which no bark had ever yet entered....Four leagues from Lake Frontenac there is an incredible Cataract or Waterfall, which has no equal. The Niagara River near this place is only the eighth of a league wide, but it is very deep in places, and so rapid above the great fall, that it hurries down all the animals which try to cross it, without a single one being able to withstand its current. They plunge down a height of more than five hundred feet, and its fall is composed of two sheets of water and a cascade, with an island sloping down. In the middle these waters foam and boil in a fearful manner.
Father Hennepin

side they built a fort and named it Fort Niagara. Marching on to Lake Erie, they built others, creating a chain of outposts which stretched from Quebec on the St. Lawrence over to the mouth of the Mississippi.

The Niagara area was to remain under the control of France for the next 80 years but English–French rivalry was on the increase and in 1759 the English, in an attempt to lay claim to the area, began a seige on Fort Niagara. The English with their Indian allies swept through the Niagara area shooting and taking many French prisoners. Eventually, the French Fort Niagara was reduced to ruins and left in the hands of the British. Activities on the east side of the river, what we now call Canada, remained unsettled, and, except for the natives that already lived there, wild and uncultivated.

Until 1774, the Niagara area enjoyed relative peace. However, as the American Revolution spread throughout the American colonies, Fort Niagara became crowded with fleeing Loyalists driven from their homes in nearby states.

At the end of this revolution the Treaty of 1783 allocated Fort Niagara to the United States. Yet the British continued to hold on to this strategic centre for a further 13 years. Eventually, many Loyalists saw the shores of Canada as a haven and a refuge and many decided to re–establish on the west side of the Niagara River at the mouth of Lake Ontario. This was the beginnings of west Niagara, later named Newark, which is now known as Niagara–on–the–Lake.

With little but their optimism and good common sense, the Town of Newark

Photographs *Eighteenth-century drills at Fort Erie (left) and at Fort Niagara (above).*

Father Hennepin passed on and after him came other French settlers: the priests, the soldiers and the traders.

A new sound was to be heard in the ancient forest—the sharp ring of steel against the tree trunks as the French cut out a portage road around the mighty cataract. At the mouth of the Niagara River on the American

began to rise from the woods. They cultivated their lands, and soon fields and orchards began to spread around the small town. Newark was soon laid out with broad streets running at right angles. Churches and civic buildings soon followed.

By 1800, 17 years after its founding, Newark was one of the busiest trading posts in Upper Canada. Nearby Queenston, with its shipping and forwarding offices, was a vital link in the transportation movement to the west. The Niagara area was a hub of activity. Yet all of this would change in the early summer of 1812.

From 1812 to 1814, the Canadian side of the Niagara River from Niagara–on–the–Lake to Fort Erie became a battleground. Bloody battles were fought at Chippawa, Lundy's Lane and Queenston Heights. Villages were laid waste and forts destroyed.

When peace came again at the end of 1814, the once prosperous Niagara was no more. The Niagara–on–the–Lake and Queenston area was no longer the hub of activity that it had once been. In 1824, the start of the Welland Canal joining Lake Erie and Ontario took away any hope of it getting on its feet again. However, the building of this waterway gave a tremendous boost to those towns along its route.

When the Welland Canal was finally opened in 1829 with a new water route between the east coast and mid–west, more people were now able to visit Niagara Falls.

In 1848 the first suspension bridge was built over the Niagara Gorge. This was soon followed by other bridges in the 1850s and trains then began to arrive daily in Niagara Falls. A new era in Niagara's history was soon to begin.

In 1765, Benjamin Franklin poked fun at the English people's lack of knowledge of the Falls by writing to a London newspaper, "The grand leap of the whale up the Fall of Niagara is esteemed, by all who have seen it, as one of the finest spectacles of Nature!"

Photographs *Terrapin Tower with three hotels in the background. View from the United States circa 1840 (above). The Niagara Falls Suspension Bridge (right), first opened in 1848.*

The only Route via
NIAGARA FALLS & SUSPENSION BRIDGE

For DETROIT, CHICAGO, SAN FRANCISCO and all points West
the GREAT WESTERN & MICHIGAN CENTRAL Ry.
Palace, Sleeping & Drawing-Room Cars between New York, Boston & Chicago without change.

The tourist era began in the late 1840s after John Roebling built his railway suspension bridge—the wonder of the age—across the gorge. Nothing like it had ever been constructed before. Critics scoffed, but Roebling's bridge did not fall down. The trains ran, the masses arrived and the carnival flourished.

Niagara Falls can boast a succession of firsts, each of which mirrors the times; the first museum in North America, the first railway suspension bridge in the world, the first use of public money to expropriate land for public parks and the first hydroelectric power development in history.

Photograph Advertisement for the Great Western & Michigan Central Railway, 1876. Courtesy of Niagara Parks Commission.

THE HONEYMOON MECCA

THE NIAGARA LEGEND
*Indian legend tells of Lelawala, a beautiful maid betrothed by her father
to a brave she despised. Rather than marry, Lelawala chose to sacrifice herself
to her true love He–No, the Thunder God, who dwelled in a cave
behind the Horseshoe Falls. She paddled the canoe into the swift current
of the Niagara River and was swept over the brink. He–No caught her as she
plummeted and together their spirits are said to live forever
in the Thunder God's sanctuary behind the falls.*

Niagara Falls' romantic magnetism has made it a honeymoon mecca. Some say it's the sexy powers of the negative ions generated at the Falls, others say it's the Falls' sheer majesty. But whatever the reason, for almost 200 years everyone from pioneers to jet–setting celebrities has been attracted by its allure.

Falling in love is not often taken that literally in the Honeymoon City. Nevertheless, Niagara Falls is synonymous with the sweetness of romance, and the tumbling water has plucked many a passionate note on the heartstrings of lovers.

"It has been said," writes Pierre Berton in his historical work *Niagara: A History of the Falls,* "that honeymooners went

Photographs *Canadian side of the Falls (left) with the Maid of the Mist. Painted by T. Benecke in 1856. Honeymooners (above and top right). A honeymoon couple (right) at the brink of the Horseshoe Falls in 1956.*

to the Falls to lose themselves in a crowd too busy contemplating the cataract to notice the billing and cooing at their elbows; that the sound of the falling water acted as an aphrodisiac; that the negative ions produced by the cascade served as a stimulant for the marriage bed; that moonlight dappling the water provided a lure to the romantic; that cataracts and waterfalls have always been associated with love, passion, obsession..."

Modern Customs

The modern custom of honeymooning at Niagara Falls, once called the bridal tour, goes back almost 200 years. This tradition began in 1801 when American aristocrats Theodosia Burr, daughter of future U.S. Vice President Aaron Burr, and Joseph Alston chose to honeymoon in Niagara Falls.

At that time, Niagara was frontier territory and the expedition from Albany, New York required nine pack horses and a train of servants to reach the three sets of waterfalls. There's no written record of their impressions, writes Dwight Whalen, author of *Lovers Guide to Niagara Falls,* and he speculates that wonders other than the falls may have absorbed too much of their attention.

But with that pilgrimage of love, a tradition was born. Three years later Jerome Bonaparte (younger brother of Napoleon) and his Baltimore–born bride, Elizabeth Patterson, made the overland trek.

At first honeymooning was limited to the wealthy. But in 1825 when the Erie Canal opened a water route between the east coast and the midwest, Niagara became accessible to middle–class lovers. Beginning in 1836, honeymooners from every class of life were travelling to Niagara by train. And by 1851, visitors could take a non–stop train from American cities to a depot only a short walk from the Falls. In Niagara's heyday, 47 trains representing ten railroads pulled into Niagara Falls, N.Y. daily.

The smallest of the three cataracts, squeezed between the American and Horseshoe Falls, was christened the Bridal Veil Falls. Superstition says that newlyweds who toss coins into its thin, shimmering cascade will reap good fortune throughout their married life.

Long before royal honeymooners proclaimed its beauty, fashionable ladies discovered Niagara Falls as a potent source of eligible young men. And, thank or blame the negative ions, in 1901, a woman demonstrated that emotion knows no boundary. This 63 year old went over the Falls in a wooden barrel in the hope, some say, that fame and fortune would capture her the man of her dreams.

In the 1920s Niagara Falls was also referred to as the "Baby City" since it was believed that more babies were conceived here than anywhere else in the world.

Whatever the season, whatever the reason, Niagara Falls is still the place to honeymoon.

Photographs *Bride and groom in Oakes Gardens (opposite). A couple (top right) enjoying a bike ride through Queen Victoria Park.*
A honeymoon couple (bottom right) in 1951 view the American Falls from a lookout in Queen Victoria Park.

15

Between October 24, 1901 and October 1, 1995, 15 people intentionally went over the Canadian Horseshoe Falls in contraptions ranging from a wooden barrel to a kayak. Ten lived to tell of their adventures, five lost their lives. Here are their stories.

Photographs 1. Annie Taylor , the first person to go over the Falls in a barrel, emerges from her barrel on October 24, 1901. 2. Bobby Leach proudly displays the barrel that he successfully used to conquer the Falls on July 25, 1911. 3. Jean Lussier on July 4, 1928, the fourth person to plunge over the Falls. 4. George Stathakis at the start of his fateful trip, July 4, 1930. 5. William "Red" Hill Jr. as he enters "The Thing" before his fatal plunge over the Canadian Horseshoe Falls on August 5, 1951. 6. William Fitzgerald (alias Nathan Boya) and a policeman examine the ball in which he went over the Falls the day after his trip on July 15, 1961 7. Karel Soucek's barrel is retrieved by the Park's Police on July 2, 1984. He was the eighth to go over the Falls. Photos 1,2,5 and 6 courtesy of the Niagara Falls Heritage Foundation.

1

3

4

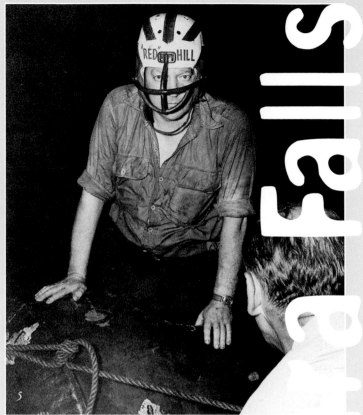

5

6

2

7

1. ANNIE TAYLOR OCTOBER 24, 1901
(SURVIVED)

Annie Taylor holds the distinction of being the first person to go over Niagara Falls in a barrel. When she made her trip she said she was 43 years of age, however, genealogical records confirm she was actually 63 years old.

This Bay City, Michigan school teacher was strapped by her assistants into a special harness in a wooden barrel. Several newspaper people were on hand as a small boat towed the barrel out into the mainstream of the Niagara River and was cut loose. Slammed by the rapids first one way, then another, Mrs. Taylor was sure she hit the rocks. Yet just 17 minutes after the plunge, her barrel drifted close enough to the Canadian shore to be hooked and dragged onto the rocks. Dazed but triumphant, the first person to conquer the mighty Falls of Niagara found the fame she sought so desperately.

Unfortunately, 20 years after her brush with death, she died destitute in Niagara Falls, New York.
On emerging from her barrel after plunging over Niagara Falls on October 24, 1901 Annie Taylor said, "No one ought ever do that again."

2. BOBBY LEACH JULY 25, 1911
(SURVIVED)

Bobby Leach, a native of Cornwall, England survived a plunge over the Horseshoe Falls in a cylindrical steel barrel on July 25, 1911. As a result of the trip, he spent six months in the hospital recuperating from numerous fractures and other injuries.

Years later, at the age of 67, Bobby Leach went on a tour with his daughter to Australia and New Zealand when tragedy struck. On April 29, 1925 while walking on a street in New Zealand, he slipped on an orange peel. After developing complications his leg had to be amputated. He contracted gangrene poisoning and died.

3. CHARLES STEPHENS JULY 11, 1920
(DIED)

Stephens, a barber from Bristol, England was the third person to go over Niagara Falls. He lost his life on July 11, 1920, after going over the Falls at approximately 8:35 a.m. All that remained were a few white staves of the barrel and Stephens's tattooed right arm. The rest of his body, attached to an anvil used as ballast for the barrel, sank to the bottom of the river.

4. JEAN LUSSIER JULY 4, 1928
(SURVIVED)

Jean Lussier, originally from Quebec and living in Niagara Falls, New York challenged the Falls on U.S. Independence Day in 1928. This machinist's successful trip was in a rubber ball. Self designed, this 1.8 metre (six-foot) ball was lined with rubber tubes filled with oxygen.

On July 4, 1928, after taking some hard knocks in the upper rapids, it skipped perfectly over the Falls. One hour later, Lussier stepped ashore below the Falls none the worse for wear.

Displaying his ball at Niagara Falls for many years, he sold small pieces of the inner tubes for fifty cents a piece.

5. GEORGE STATHAKIS JULY 4, 1930
(DIED)

This Buffalo, New York chef went over the Falls in a large wooden barrel. It is assumed he survived the plunge over the Falls but his barrel was caught behind the curtain of water and remained trapped for almost 18 hours. Finally it broke loose and was towed to shore and opened. Stathakis, with only enough oxygen for three hours, had died of suffocation. However, his pet turtle, taken along for good luck, was still alive.

6. WILLIAM "RED" HILL JR.
AUGUST 5, 1951 (DIED)

In the summer of 1951, William "Red" Hill Jr. rode over Niagara Falls in a flimsy contrivance consisting of 13 inner tubes held together with fish net and canvas straps. He referred to the contraption as "a thing." Police made no attempt to prevent the trip and thousands lined the river's edge to watch this well-publicized event.

Towed out into the Niagara River from Ussher's Creek on the Canadian side of the river, he was set adrift into the swift Niagara current. Plummeting down, the "thing" disappeared into the mist and boiling water at the base of the Falls. Seconds later a tangle of inner tubes and torn netting emerged as well as Hill's air mattress. The following day his battered body was recovered.

7. WILLIAM FITZGERALD, ALSO KNOWN AS NATHAN T. BOYA JULY 15, 1961
(SURVIVED)

Shortly before 11:00 a.m. on July 15, a large dark "ball" floated down the Niagara River and over the Falls. When retrieved by Maid of the Mist employees, the man who identified himself as Nathan Boya emerged from this 544 kg, 3 m (1,200 lb. 10-ft.) diameter rubber ball. Niagara Parks Police were there to greet him and as a result Boya has the distinction of being the first person to be charged and convicted under the Niagara Parks Act for failure to obtain "a ceremonial permit from the Niagara Parks Commission, to perform an act which congregates or is likely to congregate persons, contrary to the regulations of the Niagara Parks Act."

Boya was fined $100 and costs of $13. He gave no explanation for his trip, simply saying, "I had to do it, I wanted to do it and I am glad I did it." Today FitzGerald lives in the New York City area.

8. KAREL SOUCEK – JULY 3, 1984
(SURVIVED)

Karel Soucek, a stunt man from Hamilton, Ontario was the first Canadian to go over the Horseshoe Falls and live to tell about it.

His 2.7 m (nine-foot) long, 1.5 m (five-foot) diameter cylindrical-shaped steel barrel with fibreglass mouldings at either end was insulated with liquid foam. Equipped with a snorkel for breathing and two eye holes to look out, his trip took approximately 3.2 seconds. But he then became trapped in dangerous waters below the Falls inside his bright red barrel. After 45 minutes he was rescued by his ground crew, suffering cuts and bruises, an injury to his left arm and a chipped tooth. He was treated at the Niagara Falls General Hospital and charged by the Niagara Parks Police under the Niagara Parks Act. Later he paid a $500 fine for his stunt.

On January 19, 1985, Soucek attempted to duplicate his Falls ride from the top of the Houston Astrodome in Texas. This journey was in a wooden barrel specially designed to plunge 55 m (180 feet) into a ten-foot deep pool. Unfortunately, the barrel started to spin as it was released and it crashed onto the edges of the tank. Karel Soucek died of massive injuries. He is buried at the Drummond Hill Cemetery in Niagara Falls, Ontario.

9. STEVEN TROTTER – AUGUST 18, 1985
(SURVIVED)

Next to go over Niagara was a 22-year-old part-time bartender from Barrington, Rhode Island. In a device made of two plastic pickle barrels surrounded by large inner tubes and covered by a tarpaulin, he made his successful plunge at 8:30 a.m. on August 18, 1985.

Emerging uninjured from his home-made barrel, Trotter became the youngest man to survive the plunge. Trotter, like previous daredevils, was fined. He made a few television appearances and seemingly disappeared from the public eye until a dramatic reappearance in the summer of 1995.

Background photograph: John "David" Munday goes over the brink in his barrel on October 5, 1985.

10. JOHN "DAVID" MUNDAY OCTOBER 5, 1985 (SURVIVED)

On October 5, 1985, two months after his first attempt to conquer the Horseshoe Falls was foiled by Niagara Parks Police, John "David" Munday finally succeeded. Dressed in blue coveralls, this 48-year-old mechanic from Caistor Centre (near Hamilton, Ontario) made his trip in a two-metre (seven-foot) long, four-foot diameter, 454 kg (1,000 lb.) steel barrel. Lined with aluminum separated by foam, it was painted silver with a red maple leaf on the outside. His barrel, which included video and radio equipment, cost him $16,000 to build.

After the plunge, Munday's barrel was retrieved by his assistants below the Falls just outside the observation platform of the Table Rock Scenic Tunnels (now known as the Journey Behind the Falls). Emerging from his barrel and climbing up over the slippery rocks, he was cheered by his "crew" and a few local members of the news media. Munday was the tenth person to survive the trip. He was fined $1,500.

On July 15, 1990 Munday once again attempted to go over the Horseshoe Falls in a, "no frills" 179 kg (394 lb.) steel barrel. The barrel became stranded by low water on the brink of the Falls and was eventually fished out by a cable attached to a crane. Fined $4,375 for performing an illegal stunt on Niagara Parks Commission property, Munday said he was, "tickled pink" with the fine which could have reached the maximum penalty of $10,000. This is not the last we will hear of John "David" Munday.

11. & 12. PETER DEBERNARDI & GEOFFREY PETKOVICH – SEPTEMBER 27, 1989 (SURVIVED)

Peter DeBernardi of Niagara Falls, Ontario and Geoffrey Petkovich of Ottawa were the first to go over Niagara Falls in the same barrel. Positioned head to head in the ten-foot steel barrel, the contraption was launched into the Niagara River from the back of a truck at approximately 150 metres (492 ft.) above the Canadian Horseshoe Falls.

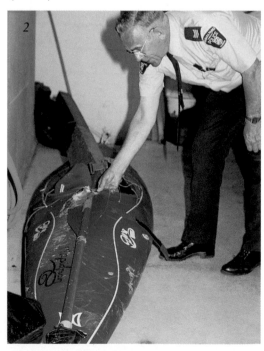

Once over the Falls, it crested and floated for several minutes close to the base. And nearing the Canadian shore, members of the daredevils' support crew snagged it with grappling hooks. When the hatch was opened, DeBernardi and Petkovich emerged with minor injuries. Climbing the bank to the Scenic Tunnels (Journey Behind The Falls), they refused medical attention and were transported to the Niagara Parks Police Office. Here they were charged with infractions under the Niagara Parks Act.

In November of the same year, Peter DeBernardi was fined $1,000 for trespassing in a prohibited area and $500 for performing a stunt in the river and gorge, a violation of the Niagara Parks Act. Earlier, Geoffrey Petkovich was fined $500.

DeBernardi is still believed to be living in Niagara Falls, Ontario while the whereabouts of Petkovich is unknown.

13. JESSIE W. SHARP JUNE 5, 1990 (DIED)

Jessie W. Sharp, a 28-year-old bachelor from Ocoee, Tennessee attempted to ride over the brink of the Horseshoe Falls in a 3.6 m (12 ft.), 16 kg (36 lb.) polyethylene kayak on June 5, 1990. Sharp, unemployed at the time, was an experienced white water kayaker. Three people who accompanied Sharp to Niagara Falls to video-tape his trip told police that Mr. Sharp had been planning the trip for several years. The person hired to video tape his trip told police that Sharp was attempting to go over the Falls in the kayak to advance his career in stunting.

Sharp did not wear a protective helmet so his face would be visible on film. He also didn't wish to wear a life jacket, believing it would interfere with his ability to escape in the event that he was caught underneath the Falls. After "shooting the Falls," he intended to continue down river through the rapids to Lewiston, New York. He had even made dinner reservations. His body has never been recovered.

14. JOHN "DAVID" MUNDAY SEPTEMBER 26, 1993 SECOND TRIP OVER THE FALLS (SURVIVED)

On September 27, 1993, John "David"

Munday became the first person to go over the Falls twice. The 56-year-old man accomplished his feat using a red and white home-made steel barrel.

At 8:35 a.m. Munday's 1.2 m (4 ft.) diameter steel ball, complete with a red maple leaf painted on the side, floated to the brink and plunged 55 m (175 ft.) into the churning waters below.

He entered the water at

4

approximately the same point he did in 1985, about 100 m (328 ft.) above the Falls. It took approximately five seconds to make the plunge. Once over the Falls, the barrel was towed by the Little Maid to the Maid of the Mist dock. Before emerging, he remained in the barrel approximately 45 minutes. He sustained no major injuries and he refused to go to the hospital. Munday was not wearing a protective helmet and there was only a five centimetre (two inch) layer of padding inside the ball to soften the impact.

Later in the year, he was fined $6,000 for his second barrel ride. He said to reporters outside the Niagara Falls Court House, "I'll never do the Canadian Horseshoe Falls again. It's always possible, the American Falls. Maybe if I had the money."

In 1995 David Munday was still working as a mechanic in Caistor Centre, Ontario.

14. STEVEN TROTTER AND LORI MARTIN JUNE 18, 1995 (SURVIVED)

Steve Trotter, a 32 year old from Fort Lauderdale, Florida went over the Falls for a second time. This time he was teamed up with friend Lori Martin, a 29-year-old woman from Atlanta, Georgia. Martin was the second woman to go over the Falls.

Their 3.6 m (12-ft.) barrel was made from two pieces of hot water heater tanks welded together and coated by Kevlar. It wieghed in at 408 kg (900 lbs.) and was reported to have cost $19,000. A Florida investment banker funded this stunt. The barrel was equipped with four oxygen tanks containing enough air to last for up to one hour and 20 minutes.

Launched shortly before 9:30 a.m. approximately 91 m (100 yds.) from the brink of the Horseshoe Falls, it went over the Falls and became lodged in a rock crevice. Members of the Niagara Falls Fire Department and Ambulance Services, along with the Niagara Parks Police, had to climb over a guard rail in the tunnels to reach the trapped barrel and secure it to shore with a line. They then undid the hatch and pulled out Martin who was wearing knee pads and

protective clothing. Trotter climbed out afterwards.

The barrel was trapped for nine days and was then removed by a crane for safety reasons. It remained with the Niagara Parks Commission for several weeks before Trotter returned to reclaim it, paying the costs that were incurred in retrieving it from below the Falls.

After being treated at the hospital, Martin and Trotter were taken into police custody and charged under the Niagara Parks Act for stunting without permission, for engaging in a prohibited act and for mischief. Bail was set at $10,000 for Trotter and $2,500 for Martin. Martin was released on bail and on July 21 she pleaded guilty and was fined $2,000 for stunting. Trotter remained in jail for almost two weeks and was fined $5,000 under the Niagara Parks Act and was ordered to pay $515 to the Greater Niagara General Hospital for medical expenses. Trespassing and mischief charges were withdrawn.

After this stunt, two people have now gone over the Falls twice and two pairs have gone over twice sharing the same barrel.

15. ROBERT OVERACKER OCTOBER 1, 1995 (DIED)

Robert Overacker, a 39-year-old man from Camarillo, California, went over the Canadian Horseshoe Falls at approximately 12:35 p.m. on a single jet ski.

Entering the Niagara River near the Canadian Niagara Power Plant, he started skiing toward the Falls. At the brink, he attempted to discharge a rocket propelled parachute that was on his back. It failed to charge. His brother and a friend witnessed the stunt.

His body was recovered by *Maid of the Mist* staff. Overacker, married with no children, became the fifteenth person since 1901 to intentionally go over the Falls in or on a device.

"I sure wouldn't want to go over them," declared U.S. Vice President Harry S. Truman responding to a reporter's question *"What do you think of the Falls?"* He visited the Falls on June 13, 1947.

Photographs: 1. John "David" Munday is interviewed at the base of the Falls after successfully going over on October 5, 1985. 2. Niagara Parks police officer examines Jessie Sharp's kayak which was retrieved after his trip on June 5, 1990. 3. Munday just minutes after emerging from his barrel on his second trip, September 26, 1993. 4. Munday's barrel is towed to the Maid of the Mist dock after going over the Falls on September 26, 1993. 5. Steve Trotter after his first plunge over the Canadian Horseshoe Falls on August 18, 1985.

5 THE MAID OF THE MIST

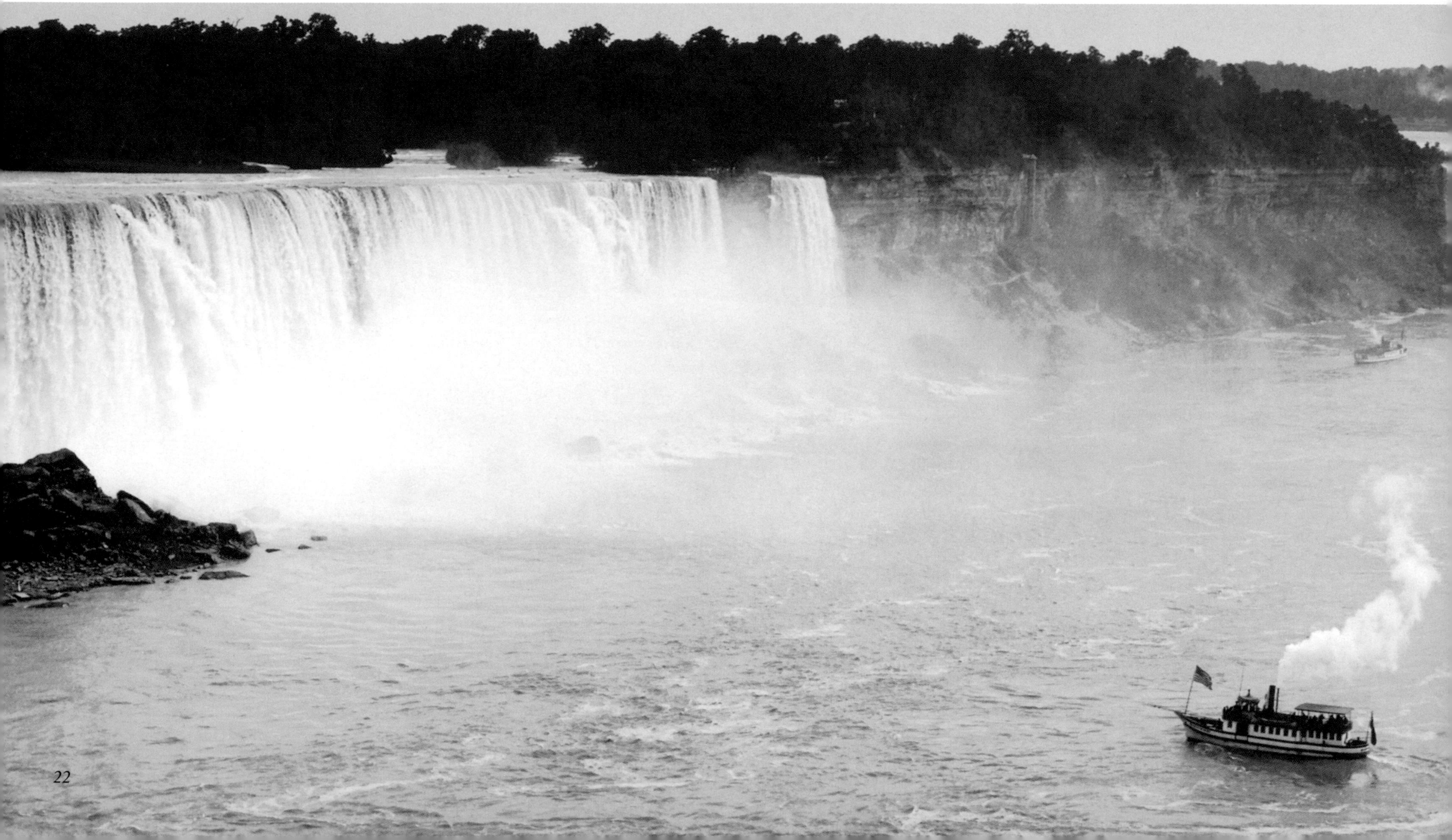

Photographs (Left) View of both Falls with Maid of the Mist in lower Niagara River, 1920's.
Maid of Mist (right) on her scenic journey.

Since there were no bridges below the lower Niagara Gorge until 1848, tourists found their way across both sides of the river by using a ferry service. As early as 1834, small boats took passengers across the lower river in approximately eight minutes. However, many tourists were apprehensive of crossing in these tiny boats.

First Maid Launched

As a result, in 1846, the Niagara Falls Ferry Association was incorporated. A side wheeler with twin smoke stacks, christened the *Maid of the Mist,* was launched amid the cheers of a large crowd on May 27, 1846.

However, this operation as a ferry service was to be short lived because in 1848 the first suspension bridge was built across the river and ferry service subsequently declined. Yet a new service arose with the Maid being used primarily for sightseeing.

Second Maid Launched

Due to its popularity, a larger and more luxurious Maid was built. On July 14, 1854, a single stacked steamed paddle wheeler was launched. Six years later, King Edward VII, during his royal visit to Niagara Falls, embarked on a trip aboard the Maid.

A number of other members of the British royal family would take similar trips on the Maid over the next 125 years.

A Wild Trip

In 1861, due to financial difficulties and an impending Civil War in the United States, the Maid was sold at a public auction. Sold to a Canadian firm on the condition it be delivered into Lake Ontario, the boat had to be piloted down the lower rapids through a 1.8 km (3 mi.) section of some of the world's wildest white water.

Captain Joel Robinson, a superior navigator, and two deck hands agreed to deliver the boat through the rapids to Lake Ontario. People said it couldn't be done, but a fee of $500 convinced the captain otherwise.

On June 6, 1861 curiosity seekers crowded the shoreline to see Robinson and his crew successfully navigate the lower Niagara rapids.

With the exception of losing a smoke stack, their trip to Queenston, Ontario was successful. But because they had started their trip from the United States and landed in Canada, a customs collector at Queenston made the crew fill out entrance and clearance papers!

A recreation of this historic trip has been captured magnificently in the film "Niagara; Miracles; Magics and Myths", shown throughout the year at the Niagara Falls Imax Theatre in Niagara Falls, Canada. Incidentally, the boat was successfully delivered to the Canadian businessman who had purchased her.

Third Maid Launched

It would not be until June of 1885 that another *Maid of the Mist* would operate tours below the Falls. This new third *Maid of the Mist* was 21.3 m (70 ft.) long, slightly smaller in length and width than her predecessor, but superior in every other respect. The Maid was built of the finest white oak with a glass enclosed cabin for her captain. She was also able to venture closer to the base of the Horseshoe Falls than the other Maids.

Fourth Maid Built

Success breeds success, and a sister ship was built in 1892 on the American landing.

Two Maids Burn

In 1938, a great ice jam below the Falls damaged the Honeymoon Bridge and threatened to destroy the two Maids in their winter berths on the Canadian shore. Ironically, they were saved from this icy ordeal only to be destroyed by a spectacular fire 17 years later. It was on April 22, 1955 that a fire from an unknown source set them ablaze. The boats were destroyed beyond repair. In less than a month a 12.2 m (40-ft.) open yacht was delivered and christened *The Little Maid*. She would serve until a new Maid was delivered later in the year.

MAID of the MIST VI

New Boats Arrive in the 1950s

A new Maid was launched on July 28, 1955. This boat was different not only because it was steel, but it was built off site. Constructed at an Owen Sound, Ontario shipyard, it was taken apart in four pieces, delivered to the Canadian dock and reassembled.

She was christened *Maid of the Mist.* An identical all-steel sister ship arrived in June of 1956. She was christened *Maid of the Mist II*, although it was the sixth vessel to bear the name, not counting the *Little Maid.* This ship would play a role in one of the most spectacular and historic events that ever took place at Niagara. Piloted by Captain Clifford Keech she rescued young seven-year-old Roger Woodward who accidently went over the Falls on July 9, 1960. His story is told in detail on page 48.

Later in 1983, this Maid was sold to the Ontario District of the United Pentecostal Church. She was refitted as a houseboat and sailed 11,265 km (7,000 mi.) to her new home in Peru. Today she continues to be used as a missionary ship on the Amazon River.

In 1971, the Maid of the Mist Corporation was purchased by James V. Glynn of nearby Lewiston, New York.

Lowered Into the Gorge
In 1972, a new *Maid of the Mist III* was delivered on a 100 ton flatbed truck from Wheatley, Ontario. Unlike previous Maids, this 65 ton vessel was lowered by two giant cranes over the Canadian Gorge to the landing below.

In 1976 a larger *Maid of the Mist IV*, able to carry 200 passengers, was lowered in a similar manner over the gorge to join her sister ship.

On June 6, 1983, the newly constructed *Maid of the Mist V* began a three-day journey from her building site in Wheatley, Ontario to the landing below the Falls. This all-steel vessel sported a double deck and was equipped to carry 300 passengers. She became the ninth and largest ship in the history of the Maid of the Mist company. Similar to the two previous Maids, she was hauled on a flatbed truck and lowered over the gorge by two giant cranes.

Seven years later, in 1990, an even bigger ship, the *Maid of the Mist VI*, was built in Port Dover, Ontario. Unlike the previous three Maids, this vessel was disassembled into four sections, hauled to Niagara Falls, lowered over the gorge and reassembled at the river's edge. This all-steel, double deck ship carries up to 600 passengers.

In 1996 four Maid of the Mists sail the Niagara River below the Falls. Depending on ice conditions in the Niagara River, the Maids can be launched for the season as early as April. They are taken out of the water each year at the end of October and must be out by November 1 when maximum water diversion for winter hydro power begins. If they were not removed, the boats would be left high and dry at the dock side.

These scenic trips continue to this day. In 1996, the *Maid of the Mist* proudly celebrates her 150th birthday.

NIAGARA'S TOWERS

Towers are not new to Niagara Falls. On the Canadian side there have been a total of 13 towers built since 1824. Those observation towers at and around Lundy's Lane served as vantage points for American tourists who came to see where, in 1814, one of the fiercest battles of the War of 1812 took place.

After the American Civil War, the popularity of the battlefield declined and the Americans switched their interests to the battlefield at Gettysburg. By 1867, there was a definite lack of American interest in the Lundy's Lane battlefield and towers.

There was also a tower called Street's Pagoda located on Cedar Island 500 m (1/4 mi.) above the Horseshoe Falls on the Canadian side. This 15-metre (50 foot) tower was made of wooden beams and covered on the outside with wooden lattice work. Some say it was built especially for the viewing pleasure of the Prince of Wales on the occasion of his visit to Niagara in 1860. Street's Pagoda did not prove to be financially successful.

Between 1833 and 1873, the most famous tower on the American side of the border was Terrapin Tower. Standing on Goat Island at the edge of the Horseshoe Falls, it was built by Judge Augustus Porter and his brother Peter Porter who owned the island. Field stones gathered in the vicinity were used to build the tower. It was round, about 14 m (45 ft.) high and 3.7 m (12 ft.) in diameter at its base and 2.8 m (8 ft.) wide at its top.

Every picture of Niagara Falls between 1833 and 1873 shows this famous landmark. It also served as a valuable way to date paintings. Considered unsafe, the building was deliberately demolished with black powder in 1873.

In the 1990s, Niagara Falls, Canada sports three towers; the Skylon, the Minolta and the Maple Leaf Tower. On the American side of the border just beside the American Falls is the Prospect Point Observation Tower.

Photographs (clockwise) The Skylon Tower; Terrapin Tower on Goat Island in 1869; the Minolta Tower; the Maple Leaf Tower.

In the mid 1830s Niagara was thought of as the most healthful place in all of North America. This was explained by early writers such as Robert Burford Esq. who said, "The agitation of the surrounding air produced by the tremendous Falls, combines with the elevation and dryness of the soil and absence of swamps, to produce this happy result."

Niagara Falls

29

THE POWER OF 7 NIAGARA

Photographs *Excavation (right) for conduits for Ontario Power Company showing Table Rock House in the background, April 8, 1910. Courtesy of Ontario Hydro Archives.*

Hydroelectric Power

The Niagara River, although only 58 kilometres (36 miles) long, is one of the world's greatest sources of hydroelectric power. During its short course, the river drops 99 m (326 ft.) between Lake Erie and Lake Ontario with the greatest portion of the drop, approximately 52 m (170 ft.), occurring at the Falls.

Water was first diverted from the Canadian side of the Niagara River for the generation of electricity in 1893. A small 2,200 kilowatt (kW) plant was built just above the Horseshoe Falls to power an electric railway between the historic communities of Queenston and Chippawa. However, the first five years of this century would see rapid power development on the Canadian side of the river with three power generating plants all under construction.

The Canadian Niagara Power Company

In 1899, in an agreement between the Niagara Parks Commission and the Canadian Niagara Power Company, the company was allowed to build a generating plant above the Falls for the purpose of diverting water from the river to produce electricity. The Canadian Niagara Power Company opened on January 1, 1905 and began to produce 100,000 hp. The plant is still in operation in 1996.

Ontario Power Company

In 1900, a similar agreement was reached with the Ontario Power Company for the development of electrical power on the Canadian side of the Niagara River. This plant was built in the Niagara Gorge below the Canadian Horseshoe Falls where water was diverted through three large conduits from above the Falls.

The powerhouse is still operating and produces 125,000 hp.

The Electrical Development Company of Ontario, Ltd.

Three years later on January 29, 1903, an agreement was formed by the Niagara Parks Commission and the Electrical Development Company of Ontario Ltd. to construct a plant above the Falls on what was previously the river bed. The main tail–race tunnel was 610 m (2,000 ft.) in length and about 11.5 m (33 ft.) in diameter discharging water behind the Canadian Horseshoe Falls. Built of Indiana Limestone, the cornerstone of this Italian Renaissance style building was laid in 1906 and power was first delivered on November 21, 1906. The powerhouse had a capacity of 137,500 hp.

The powerhouse was closed in 1974. Today it sits idle in Queen Victoria Park with no plans finalized for its fate.

Today, the churning river provides the driving force for almost 2,000,000 kW of electricity from a number of power plants on the Canadian side. The three largest are Sir Adam Beck–Niagara Generating Station Nos. 1 and 2 and the nearby pumping station. Studies are under way on the building of a 700,000 kW third station with a proposed in–service date of 1998.

Sir Adam Beck No. 1

Called the Queenston–Chippawa development when construction began in 1917, the Sir Adam Beck–Niagara Generating Station No. 1 was for many years the largest hydroelectric plant in the world. To use the maximum fall of the river, water had to be diverted from an intake 3.2 km (1.9 mi.) above the Horseshoe Falls to the plant at the base of the Niagara Gorge. To accomplish this, hydro engineers built an open canal 20 km (16 mi.) long from Chippawa across the country to a triangular basin called a forebay on the escarpment more than 90 m (270 ft.) above the Niagara River. From the forebay, giant penstocks (tubes) carry the water to the powerhouse at the river's edge below. The powerhouse accommodating the generating, transforming and control equipment rises more than halfway up the cliff to a height of 55 m (165 ft.). And with a total of ten generating units, the plant has an installed capacity of 414,650 kW.

Sir Adam Beck No. 2

Construction of this station began in 1951 beside the first plant. As it was not feasible to interrupt surface traffic to build another open canal, two underground tunnels were built to carry 68 million litres of water a minute from Chippawa to the forebay. With a finished diameter of 14 m (45 ft.), the parallel tunnels are nine kilometres (5.6 mi) long and pass directly under the City of Niagara Falls, often at a depth of 101 m (323 ft.).

Opened in 1954, Beck No. 2 now houses 16 generating units and is almost twice as long as the Beck No. 1 station. The plant has an installed capacity of 1,223,600 kW.

Pumping–Generation Station

During periods of peak power demands, the 176,700 kW pumping–generating station contributes to the peak electrical output of Beck No. 2. During off–peak hours, water is pumped into a reservoir covering more than 300 hectares (494 acres). With the pumps reversed and acting as turbo–generators, the water is released at peak periods to produce electricity. The station has six pumping–generating units, all of which were in service by 1958.

Sir Adam Beck No. 3 Proposal
Ontario Hydro announced in mid–1988 that it would proceed with studies towards developing a third hydraulic station. This is to be located at the base of the cliff between Beck No. 1 station and the Lewiston–Queenston bridge with its headgates inside the pumped storage reservoir. The output of the proposed station, which is part of the development of the province's remaining hydroelectric resources, would be 700,000 kilowatts from two units.

Water to the Beck No. 3 station would be supplied to the pumped storage reservoir by construction of two tunnels under the existing tunnels from Chippawa. Environmental regulatory approvals are now being sought.

Used by a combined Canada/United States population of more than 1,000,000 people, the waters of the Niagara River are used for a wide range of purposes:

❑ A source of drinking water;
❑ A source of industrial process and cooling water;
❑ A source of hydroelectric power generation;
❑ A tourist attraction;
❑ A recreational attraction;
❑ A receiver of discharges and wastes from industries and municipalities along its shores

THE TOURIST

Photographs (left) Canadian Niagara waterfront as seen from the Queenston Hotel in September, 1927. (above) The Canadian side with Oakes Garden Theatre in the foreground, taken in the late 1930s. Blondin (right) carries his manager on his back across the Niagara Gorge in 1859.

Tourism Is Born

By the 1860s a new form of commerce had developed in Niagara: the "tourist business." In fact, this booming trade quickly became overbearing to many. Oscar Wilde, the nineteenth century author and wit, made a number of observations when he visited the Falls in January of 1882. He said, "Niagara Falls is endless water falling the wrong way." But perhaps his most memorable comment was "Niagara Falls must be a bride's second greatest disappointment."

Some writers described how "hackmen" would meet the tourists as they arrived at the railway station and attempt to get them on their "hacks" to take them on a tour of the area. Persistent, these individuals did not like to take no for an answer. One writer of the 1860s warned "The first thing to do on your arrival is to get rid of the hackmen, whose vociferations are enough to drown ten Niagaras, for dispose of them you must if you would not have them following you like shadow from dawn to dewy eve."

Of course, if you were unlucky enough to get into one of these carriages the hackman would suggest points of interest, steer you in that direction and eventually obtain a large commission from the owner of the establishment for bringing you to their business.

Another trick was for a photographer to take a photo of an unsuspecting tourist. Before the poor tourist could decline, he was presented with a finished photo and a bill for four or five dollars.

Stunting Begins

Another activity that would draw thousands to Niagara was performances by "funambulists," tightrope walkers who would "walk the line" across the Niagara River gorge.

The first person to tightrope walk across the gorge between Canada and the United States was Jean François Gravelet, or the Great Blondin. He crossed on a five centimetre (two inch) Manila hemp tightrope suspended 61 m (200 ft.) over the Niagara Gorge. To the astonishment of the crowd of thousands, this 35 year old made the trip several times.

On one trip, he paused half way, lowered a cord to the deck of the *Maid of the Mist* waiting below, drew up a bottle of wine and cavalierly drank the contents before finishing his walk.

Blondin was to repeat this walk many times in 1860. He did it pushing a wheel barrel; with a sack on his head; on a bicycle; and with his arms and legs in manacles. On another occasion, he carried his manager across on his back, and yet another time, he pushed a cook stove to the centre of the rope, prepared a meal and lowered it to the passengers on the *Maid of the Mist*.

After Blondin's spectacular feats, many other funambulists would perform above the gorge for years to come. Blondin's feats still stand out in the history of Niagara Falls.

It would not be until 1901 that tightrope walking would be replaced by barrel riding over Niagara. By the early 1880s, change was already just around the corner.

Photographs *(clockwise from top left) The voyage of the* Maid of the Mist; *Postcard showing the visit of King George VI and Queen Elizabeth to the Falls; the Duke and Duchess of York on the* Maid of the Mist; *Sir Winston Churchill and his daughter Mary visit Queenston Heights Restaurant in 1944.*

Photographs *(clockwise from left) Visitors to Table Rock in 1932; Princess Diana and Princes William and Harry enjoy orange juice aboard the* Maid of the Mist *in October, 1991. Photo by George Bailey; The Niagara Spanish Aero Car, a popular tourist attraction, crosses over the Niagara Whirlpool; Princess Margaret on her tour of Niagara Falls in 1958.*

Wish you were here

As we have seen, the early 1900s witnessed power development, daredevils, growth as the honeymoon capital of the world and the development of a world-class public park. Yet by the end of the nineteenth century, the face of Niagara Falls had taken on a new glow.

In addition to the barrel riders who challenged the Falls, there were those who challenged the lower Whirlpool Rapids—one of the fastest flowing stretches of inland waters in the world. Between 1886 and 1987, 21 people went through the Whirlpool

Rapids in barrels. Many made this trip more than once. Bobby Leach, who also went over the Falls successfully, made four trips through the rapids between 1898 and 1911. And three members of Niagara Falls' Hill family made seven trips through the rapids between 1930 and 1956.

Four individuals each made a trip through the rapids before conquering Niagara in a barrel. Bobby Leach who was the first, conquered the Falls in 1911. William "Red" Hill Jr. lost his life when he attempted to go over Niagara Falls in 1951. Karl Soucek challenged the Whirlpool Rapids on June 11, 1977 and Dave Munday made his rapids trip on October 13, 1987. These last two trips were successful but were taken without the permission of the Niagara Parks Commission

who, for many years, refused to allow stunters to perform acts of this nature on their property.

However, there have been two exceptions. In 1981, the Niagara Parks Commission granted permission to the ABC television network to allow four people to go through the Whirlpool Rapids in kayaks. The Commission felt the venture was a sporting event performed by professionals and not a stunt. The trips were successful.

In the late 1980s, the Commission gave approval to the producers of a new Imax film to navigate a vessel from below the Falls through the lower Whirlpool rapids; a recreation of a trip made through the lower rapids in 1861. The trip took place without incident. At that time, the second *Maid of the*

Mist was delivered down the Niagara River into Lake Ontario after being purchased by a Montreal firm. That trip also went off without incident and a recreation of this can be seen in the Imax film *Niagara Miracles, Magics and Myths* shown at the Niagara Falls Imax Theatre.

With the improvement of roads and the increasing popularity of the automobile, Niagara Falls became a popular motoring destination in the 1920s and 30s. Families would pile into their new status symbol, the automobile, and take a motoring trip to Niagara. Many camped out at two major campgrounds in the Clifton Hill and

Fallsview areas of Niagara. But by the early 1950s, these sites were quickly replaced with a more modern type of accommodation—the motel.

During the Depression of the 1930s up until the end of the Second World War, Niagara Falls, like many other tourist destinations, showed a marked decline in the number of visitors. However, things were to change in the late 1940s.

Beginning in the late forties, Niagara Falls entered a new era of prosperity; there was the development of roadways, the increased popularity of the automobile and the development of the Niagara Parks Commission.

Lundy's Lane, once a residential area, began to sprout motels, shopping plazas, restaurants and supermarkets. The improvements carried out by the Niagara Parks Commission also had a positive effect on the number of people who visited. Niagara Falls was on the verge of change.

In the early 1950s, Niagara gained a worldwide reputation as the honeymoon

Marineland, developed into a world-class attraction featuring marine life, animals and outdoor rides. A new Imax Theatre opened and today it continues to feature popular Imax films. An outdoor amusement park, Maple Leaf Village, opened on nearby Clifton Hill. Several new full-service hotels were also built in Niagara Falls, Canada.

Photographs (From far left) Marilyn Monroe in the Table Rock Retail Store, 1952; John Candy and Rhea Perlman with director Michael Moore at Niagara Falls for the filming of the 1993 comedy Canadian Bacon. Photo courtesy of Ontario Film Development Corp.; Christopher Reeve and Margot Kidder on location for Superman II. Aquatic thrills at Marineland.

Capital of the world with the film "Niagara." Released in 1952, it featured Marilyn Monroe at Niagara on her honeymoon. And for many years following the film, Niagara Falls, Canada was the fashionable place to honeymoon.

Niagara Falls, Canada remains a popular destination for the filming of major motion pictures. In addition to movies, dozens of television commercials are also shot on location here.

A New Tourism Era Begins

By the early 1960s, observation towers once again began to appear in Niagara Falls. In July of 1962, the Seagram Tower, now known as the Minolta Tower, opened in the Fallsview area. This tower included an observation section and restaurants. Then, in 1964, the Skylon Tower opened featuring outdoor observation areas as well as a stationary restaurant and a dining room that revolved high above the Falls.

During the 1960s Niagara Falls, Canada boasted many new attractions: three wax museums, helicopter rides over the Falls, an Indian Village, an exhibition of replicas of the British Crown Jewels, an antique auto museum, Ripley's Believe It Or Not Museum, the Age of Flight Museum and Marine Wonderland. Some of these attractions are still operating in the 1990s.

By all accounts, the 1960s were good years for attracting visitors to Niagara. These prosperous years continued until the early 1980s when a worldwide recession once again stemmed the flow of visitors to Niagara Falls.

Although development was slow in the 1980s, new attractions did appear. The original Marine Wonderland, now

THE PARKS

Photographs *The Floral Clock (below) is one of Niagara's favourite photo spots today. (Right) Strolling through Oakes Garden Theatre, Queen Victoria Park in 1952.*

By the early 1880s, both sides of the Falls were overun by hackmen, making it almost impossible to view the natural wonder of Niagara Falls without an unwelcome interruption. Governments on both sides of the Falls realized they had to do something and they had to do it quickly.

The Americans were first to establish a public park around Niagara and in 1885 a New York State Reservation at Niagara Falls would become a reality. To do so, in 1880, a bill was brought before the legislature of New York State to authorize the acquisition of lands for a state reservation at Niagara Falls. This new reservation was formally opened to the public on July 15, 1885. From that point on most people travelled to Niagara Falls, New York where they experienced little interference on their visit.

Tourism on the British side, as it was then known, began to dwindle. However, the wheels were still turning, albeit slowly, to establish a public park in Niagara Falls, Ontario, Canada. The formation of The Niagara Parks Commission would take place on March 30, 1885.

Ontario's Niagara Parks
When The Niagara Parks Commission was established in 1885, two primary goals were set; the Parks should be financially self–supporting and the Parks should provide public access to all grounds and recreation activities, where possible, without a fee.

Believe it or not, at the end of the twentieth century, the Niagara Parks Commission still accepts no taxes, receives no grants or handouts of any kind, and admission to their parklands remains free.

One of the main reasons the parks continue to be self-financed is that they operate all commercial establishments themselves within the parks system. Restaurants, snack bars, gift shops, parking lots, everything but the *Maid of the Mist* boats, are operated directly by The Niagara Parks Commission. This not only eliminates the middle person margin, it also enables the Parks Commission to maintain strict control over the quality of goods and services being sold while at the same time retaining the profits. The Commission also receives rent from the hydro facilities that have built generating stations on parks property.

Each year, the gardens explode with colourful golden daffodils. And once the daffodils have faded, brightly coloured roses bloom along with over 100,000 bedding plants supplied by the Commission's own greenhouses.

Another main reason for visiting the Falls is to enjoy the immaculate parklands operated by The Niagara Parks Commission. These extend 56 km (35 mi.) along the Niagara River from Lake Erie to Lake Ontario and offer many things to see and do. Travelling the Niagara Parkway from lake to lake is a wonderful drive any time of the day or any day of the week.

The Niagara Parkway

At Fort Erie, the southern end of the Niagara Parkway, there is historic Fort Erie, painstakingly restored to the days of the War of 1812–14. During the summer months, guards in period costume stand sentry duty while others conduct tours of the fort.

Travelling north towards the Falls, historic points of interest are clearly marked by plaques. Closer to the Falls themselves, visitors are struck by a mass of colourful gardens. A visit to the Niagara Parks Greenhouse, open free of charge year-round, offers the names of many of these flowers.

One of the more popular Niagara Parks attractions "Journey Behind the Falls," formerly Table Rock Scenic Tunnels, is at the brink of the Canadian Horseshoe Falls. Here, visitors don a yellow raincoat and take an elevator to tunnels passing in front of and behind the Falls. Later, a trip aboard one of the *Maid of the Mist* boats 500 m (1/4 mi.) north of the tunnels will ensure memories that last a lifetime.

This is the area where, at night throughout the year, the Falls are illuminated with the colours of the rainbow.

Travelling north along the Parkway

Photographs (Above) Tourists visit the Table Rock Scenic Tunnels and Observation Plaza, 1953. (Right) Some of the over 100,000 bedding plants that are presently grown in The Niagara Parks Commission's own greenhouses.

Niagara Falls

NIAGARA PARKS BOTANICAL GARDENS

are two other popular Niagara Parks attractions: The Great Gorge Adventure, a white water boardwalk; and the Niagara Spanish Aero Car, where visitors actually travel above the Niagara Whirlpool.

Continuing north is the popular Whirlpool Public Golf Course. Hikers will want to make a stop at the Niagara Glen, across from the golf course, and descend to the bottom of the gorge.

Just beyond the Glen is the Niagara Parks Botanical Gardens, site of the School of Horticulture. Parking and admittance to these botanical gardens are free although there will be a fee to enter the new Butterfly Conservatory found on the grounds. This is scheduled to open in the fall of 1996.

Not far beyond these gardens just adjacent to the lilacs is the Niagara Parks Floral Clock. Inspired by the famous floral clock built in 1903 in Princes St. Gardens in Edinburgh, Scotland, this is one of Niagara's favourite photographic backgrounds. The huge face on the clock measures some 12.2 m (40 ft.) in diameter.

Continuing north is the Queenston Heights Park, an immaculately groomed park and once the site of one of the most famous battles of the War of 1812–14. On the grounds, there is a tall monument to Sir Isaac Brock who was the British hero of that battle.

Descending down the Niagara Escarpment, one is struck by the tranquillity of the countryside. Orchards on the west side of the parkway burst with peaches, apples or pears in season while grapes flourish in some of North America's finest vineyards. Also below the escarpment in the Village of Queenston is the Mackenzie Heritage printery. It is the only museum in Canada devoted to displaying historic presses from the past 500 years.

Continuing towards Niagara-on-the-Lake there is a grand, old, Georgian style home known as McFarland House. The Niagara Parks Commission invites you to visit this historic home for a minimal fee. Playgrounds and picnic pavilions are also located here.

Just past McFarland house is the first capital of Upper Canada, Niagara–on–the–Lake, famous for the popular Shaw Festival theatres. Nearby, anchoring the north Niagara Parkway, is Fort George.

Photographs The Niagara Parks Botanical Gardens (page 45). Niagara Parks Greenhouse (page 46, top left). The Mackenzie Heritage Printery (page 46, bottom left). Niagara's orchards (near right) offer some of the finest produce in Ontario. The Living Water Wayside Chapel (far right) on the Lower Niagara Parkway. A vibrant summer scene (below) along Niagara Falls.

British politician Sir Winston Churchill, travelling by automobile along the Niagara Parkway between Niagara Falls and Queenston in 1944 said, "This is the prettiest Sunday afternoon drive in the world." He made the comment on a Saturday.

Perhaps one of the most miraculous stories ever told took place at Niagara Falls on Saturday afternoon, July 9, 1960. A man from Niagara Falls, New York took two children for a boat ride in the upper Niagara River. The boat developed motor trouble, capsized into the river and all three were thrown into the upper rapids. The man went over the Falls and was killed.

At the same time, the 17-year-old girl was plucked 6 m (20 ft.) from the very edge of the Falls and her seven-year-old brother, wearing only a life jacket and a bathing suit, went over the Canadian Horseshoe Falls. He came out alive to tell his story. His name was Roger Woodward.

Luckily, one of the scenic Maid of the Mist boats was just making its turn below the Falls when one of the crew spotted the bright orange life jacket. The veteran Captain Clifford Keech, manoeuvred his boat so that the crew could pick up the boy on the starboard side. After two unsuccessful

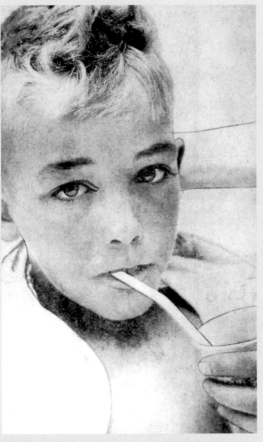

throws, a life preserver landed within reach of the crying youngster. Lifted safely on board the vessel, Roger mumbled his concern about his sister. Within the hour, word spread of this Niagara miracle. Roger was whisked to the Greater Niagara General Hospital in Niagara Falls, Ontario where he remained for three days with a slight concussion.

Another miracle was occurring at the brink of the Horseshoe Falls on the American side at Terrapin Point. Seventeen-year-old Deanne Woodward was being furiously swept towards the brink of the Falls. Hundreds stood at the brink of the Falls almost paralysed with concern for the plight of this young girl.

Two men, both from New Jersey but unknown to each other, sprang into action. John R. Hayes, a truck driver and an auxiliary police officer from Union, New Jersey climbed over the rail, stretched out his arm and pleaded with Deanne to kick harder. Deanne later said that his pleading voice

made her swim harder and she caught his thumb just before going over the Falls.

Fearful the current would break his hold on the young girl, he shouted for help. Climbing over the railing, John Quattrochi of Pennsgrove, New Jersey came to his rescue and the two pulled the frightened teenager to safety. Once on land Deanne's concern was also for her brother. Quietly, John Quattrochi whispered, "Pray for him."

With only a cut hand, Deanne was rushed to a hospital in Niagara Falls, New York where she learned of her brother's miraculous fate. The body of the man who had taken them on a boat ride, Jim Honeycutt, was freed from the depths of the Niagara River four days later.

Roger Woodward returned to Niagara Falls, Ontario on the thirtieth anniversary of the accident and spoke to the congregation at the Glengate Alliance Church. The audience was hushed as the 37-year-old told how the 3.7 m (12 ft.) aluminum

'I Went Over Head First' Boy's Nightmare Plunge

WAVE HITS, TURNS CRAFT

Three Sister Islands

SECOND WAVE OVERTURNS IT AT BEGINNING OF THE RAPIDS

Goat Island

THREE OCCUPANTS SWEPT HELPLESSLY TOWARDS THE FALLS, MAN DISAPPEARS

GIRL CARRIED CLOSE TO SHORE

Horseshoe Falls

BOY CARRIED SOME 15 FT. OUT

RESCUERS CLIMB RAIL O LEDGE AT RIVER EDGE, ACH OUT AND GRAB GIRL

BOY DROPS 162 FEET

BOY POPS UP LIKE A CORK. SEEN FROM BOAT

BOY GRABS LIFE RING. SAVED BY CREW

Niagara Falls, Ontario

fishing boat equipped with a 7 1/2 horsepower motor was caught in the fast flowing current, capsizing after hitting a shoal and breaking a pin in the engine.

Recalling his thoughts from the rapids he said, "For me there was initially pure panic, I was scared to death. I can remember going through the rapids and being thrown against the rocks and being bounced around like a toy in the water and being beaten up pretty badly. My panic very quickly shifted to anger and the anger was from seeing people running frantically up and down the shoreline and wondering why they wouldn't come out and rescue me."

Roger Woodward then said that after fear and anger came peace. "There was a time I thought I was going to die and my seven years of life literally passed before me and I started thinking what my parents would do with my dog and my toys and had really given up at that point and felt I was going to die that afternoon."

Roger Woodward did not die that afternoon and has made several trips with his family to Niagara since the miraculous incident.

In 1994 Roger Woodward and his sister Deanne Woodward Simpson once more travelled to Niagara Falls to retell their story on a half hour Canadian television special. Joining Roger and his sister were the gentlemen, now both in their eighties, who rescued Deanne from above the Falls. For Deanne it was an extremely emotional meeting. She had not seen both gentlemen in over 30 years, nor had she since stood at the edge of the Falls that had almost claimed both her life and that of her brother.

Reflecting on the accident years later, Roger Woodward said, "It wasn't the hand of fate, it wasn't the hand of luck, it wasn't the spirit of Lelawala, it was the spirit of the living God that saved my life that day and saved my sister and gave us hope that one day we would come to know him."

Photographs (Left to right) Roger Woodward at the Greater Niagara Falls General Hospital after being rescued; this aerial of Horseshoe Falls appeared in the Telegram on July 11, 1960 and reconstructs the dramatic fall; John Quattrochi, Roger Woodward, Deanne Simpson (Woodward) and John R. Hayes meet at the Falls in September, 1994.

THE OLD SCOW

ONE OF THE MOST DRAMATIC RESCUES THAT EVER TOOK PLACE AT NIAGARA FALLS OCCURRED ON AUGUST 7, 1918.

It featured a father of five, a salty Swedish sailor, a couple of cannons, a Niagara River hero, a creaking old scow, and several intrepid souls who, throughout one long night, risked life and limb to save a pair of men stranded just 307.7 m (1,000 ft.) from the brink of the Canadian Horseshoe Falls.

Today, all that's left to mark the incident, which drew worldwide attention at the time, is the shell of the rusty, deteriorated scow, still aground in the rapids just above the Falls. River watchers from the air tell us the east side of this scow has crumpled and fallen away. However, the major section of the haul remains intact, filling our minds with

questions about how it got to such a precarious position.

As the story goes, this old mud scow was moored to a tug by three supposedly strong cables. But late in the work day, these cables gave way to the weight of the scow. They snapped and the vessel madly surged towards the Falls. On board the ill–fated vessel was 40-year-old James H. Harris and a Swedish sailor, 51-year-old Gustav Lofberg. Both Buffalo natives were aboard as part of the dredging crew. Lofberg had been a sailor most of his life and had narrowly survived an earlier close call on Lake Superior when several men drowned in a vicious Great Lakes storm.

Later, Lofberg told reporters that his first words to Harris as they neared the waterfall were, "By God, we are lost!" But he quickly fell back on his sailor's resourcefulness. Trying to slow the scow, he and Harris manhandled a huge concrete anchor overboard. Weighing close to a ton, it seemed to briefly slow the scow down, yet the vessel continued to roll towards the Falls.

Finally, within sight of the lip of the waterfall, the quick-thinking men succeeded in opening one of the bottom dumping doors. This slowed the vessel, gradually filling it with water and it sank in the shallow water where it sits today.

Those on shore who witnessed the impending tragedy tried to help. In an attempt to rescue the men, some soldiers on the Canadian side of the shore floated workbenches out into the river with shore–anchor lifelines attached. These attempts were unsuccessful.

Today, a similar accident could be resolved with a quick helicopter rescue, but in 1918 the men found themselves in a potentially fatal situation. Military officials working from the roof of the Canadian Niagara Power Plant, just above the Horseshoe Falls, fired a line towards the teetering scow with the thought of running a breeches– buoy rig to the men. The cannon was not powerful enough and it fell short.

The rescuers then sent for a larger gun from the U.S. Coast Guard Station at Old Fort Niagara on the American side of the river. This time the fire power was adequate. The second shot fell directly across the bow, which was almost underwater. Lofberg made the line fast but there was still no chance of rescue until morning.

The life-savers, according to contemporary accounts, worked by searchlight while trying to string a back–line in an attempt to untangle the existing one. Great crowds cheered them on. At this point, the stranded men's thin thread of hope had become hopelessly snarled.

William "Red" Hill, patriarch of the famous family of Niagara River men, then came to the rescue. Hill already held two Carnegie metals for daring rescues in the Niagara. Guided only by searchlights, he scrambled out of the gorge in a basket rigging and untangled the fouled rescue line.

Above the waterfall, the two men shivered through the terrifying night, trying to catch snatches of sleep and to forget they were only a short distance from death.

At about 8:30 the next morning, a breeches buoy reached the scow. Lofberg helped put Harris in the harness device first. Once he was safely on shore, it was Lofberg's turn to make the trip amid the cheers of thousands of spectators lined up on the bank since dawn.

The dredging company thoughtfully gave both men the next day off. In 1995, the $35,000 scow continues to sit where it sank in 1918 intriguing many of the visitors who each year ask, "What's the story behind the old scow in the river?"

WHIRLPOOL REVERSAL PHENOMENON

All of the water flowing over Niagara Falls madly rushes towards the Whirlpool where a phenomenon occurs.

During normal times, when no water is being diverted above the Falls for power purposes, the water enters the pool and is carried past the river outlet on the right. It then circulates like most whirlpools, counter–clockwise around the pool. However, when the water is low, due to diversion above the Falls, the Whirlpool shows no circular motion and is a "whirlpool" by name only. The flow becomes clockwise only when the flow of the river goes below 17,500 m3/sec. (62,000 c.f.s.).

This Whirlpool Reversal Phenomenon has been occurring since the early 1960s when more water was diverted to produce electricity. During normal flow, the rush of water enters the pool and is carried past the river outlet on the right. It circulates in a counterclockwise direction from 6 o'clock, past 12 to 9 o'clock, then it dives under the incoming stream and emerges at the outlet in dark, boiling slugs before flowing down river.

At times of low water when the Niagara River flow goes below 17,500 m3/sec (62,000 cfs), the direction of flow in the Whirlpool becomes clockwise. This usually occurs each winter between November first and April first when there is an increase in the amount of water diverted through the tunnels above the Falls for electric power generation. The water coming into the Whirlpool is directed to the Canadian side under the influence of the sandstone ridge which lies under the entrance. At these times it shows a clockwise rotation.

51

Winter brings an added dimension of beauty to Niagara. The mist and spray from the Falls, drifting with the coldest winds of winter, spray nearby buildings, lamp posts and trees and create fantastic ice sculptures. A bright sun and a clear blue sky, made a deeper blue by the contrasting white snow, turn these ice sculptures into priceless pieces of art.

During the coldest months of January and February, great ice mountains, formed by the ice floating down the Niagara River from Lake Erie over the Falls, create ice bridges in the basin below the Falls. Sometimes accumulated ice here rises as high as 30 m (100 ft.). Complementing the scene, usually near the edge of the Falls, are long crystal icicles.

The most spectacular ice bridges were seen below the Falls prior to the 1950s. Before then, half of the water flowing over the Falls in the winter was not diverted for the creation of hydroelectric power.

In fact, it was not uncommon from the mid 1800s to the early 1900s for people to walk out on the ice bridge from both sides of the river. And by the late 1880s this was an established tourist attraction. Bright sunny afternoons were particularly favourable and many people would spend all day sliding down the ice mounds found just below the American Falls.

Photographs *The winter season at the Falls (left) brings with it a special beauty. Table Rock in the 1860s (right).*

Photographs (Below) Burrel Hecock is trapped on a piece of ice as he drifts down river to his death on February 4, 1912.
(Right) The collapsed Honeymoon Bridge taken from the American side on January 27, 1938.

Other more enterprising individuals would set up small shacks in the middle of the ice bridge and sell hot drinks and alcohol.

Ice Bridge Tragedy

Fun on the ice was to continue until 1912 when tragedy struck. On the perfect afternoon of February 4, 1912, hundreds of sightseers were on the ice bridge in the middle of the Niagara River. Suddenly, like an earthquake, the ice bridge started to break up. Everyone frantically made their way to shore except for three people. Mr. and Mrs. Eldridge Stanton of Toronto and Burrel Hecock of Cleveland were stranded on different pieces of ice. Word of their predicament spread quickly. Although brave attempts were made to rescue these stranded victims, all three lost their lives when the ice flows swept down the Niagara River and broke apart, sending them to their watery graves.

After this tragedy, a ban was established restricting anyone from going on the ice bridge. This law still exists today.

Honeymoon Bridge Collapse

Two exciting days in January of 1938 yet again attracted worldwide attention.

A combination of cold weather and a warm south-west wind sent vast masses of Lake Erie ice plunging down the upper Niagara River and over the two cataracts forming another stupendous ice jam. This build up of ice on Tuesday, January 25, 1938 shattered the docks of the Maid of the Mist, and crumpled the Maid of the Mist caretaker's home. The loud humming of the great generators in the Ontario Power Generating Plant were stopped when they were buried by great heaps of ice. An even greater tragedy was about to happen.

Ice began to accumulate against the lower girders of the Falls View Bridge. It was feared the Honeymoon Bridge, as it was also popularly known, could not withstand the massive ice build up. All traffic was stopped on the bridge at approximately 9:15 a.m. on January 26. The story of the bridge's impending doom travelled quickly and within hours, crowds of people stood by waiting for the moment when tons of steel would go crashing down onto the ice bridge below.

At 4:10 p.m. on Thursday, January 27, a crushing force of massive ice ended the bridge's 40 years of life high above the waters All that remained was a steely "W", the shape created when it crashed onto the ice bridge below.

There were no injuries in this spectacular crash and sightseers flocked daily to see what the forces of nature had created. When the mild weather arrived, this mighty structure sank to the bottom of Niagara.

In 1941, the new Rainbow Bridge was built just north of the Honeymoon Bridge. To ensure its safety, the girders were situated much higher above the level of the Niagara River.

Ice Bridge, Niagara Falls.

Other Spectacular Ice Bridges

Massive ice bridges were recorded during the winters of 1880, 1883, 1888, 1899 and 1909. Niagara Falls and several other cities were in darkness for one night as a result of the 1909 ice bridge. The accumulation of ice in early April of that year forced the closing down of the Ontario Power Company. Heavy damage was done along the lower Niagara River with all boathouses between Queenston and Niagara–on– the–Lake smashed.

The suspension bridge at Lewiston, ordinarily 18 m (60 ft.) above the water, was only 7.5 m (25 ft.) from the ice mounds in the river. The Great Gorge Railway tracks were buried under ice and all poles and wires were torn down.

The Day Niagara Stopped Flowing

Another example of winter's mighty power was recorded on March 29, 1848 when both the Niagara River and the Falls stopped flowing. The cause of this phenomenon was the accumulating of ice at the eastern end of Lake Erie which choked the entrance of the Niagara River.

People who lived near the Falls were awakened in the middle of the night by the silence of Niagara. Some went to church fearing the end of the world. When reality set in, others bravely ventured out into the middle of the river above the Falls where they retrieved bayonets, swords and even a few skeletons. One person drove a horse and buggy from Goat Island on the American side out into the middle of the river. With a crew of men and a logging cart, he gathered a large quantity of pine timber.

Niagara flowed once more on the night of March 30 when, in the middle of the night, the wind shifted and the mass of ice at the mouth of the Niagara River was released.

Ice bridges are not as severe in the 1990s for several reasons: the winters have not been as cold as those of the nineteenth century; and each winter, the Ontario Hydro & Power Authority of the State of New York installs an ice boom across the upper end of the Niagara River to prevent these ice jams. Spanning the eastern end of Lake Erie, there have been no major ice jams since its installation in 1964–65. Lastly, since the early 1950s, there has been less water going over the Falls due to the diversion of water for power purposes.

Although not as spectacular as the ice bridges of earlier years, the ice bridges of the 1990s are beautiful to observe. On a cold winter day, with bright sunshine above, the scene at Niagara is not to be missed.

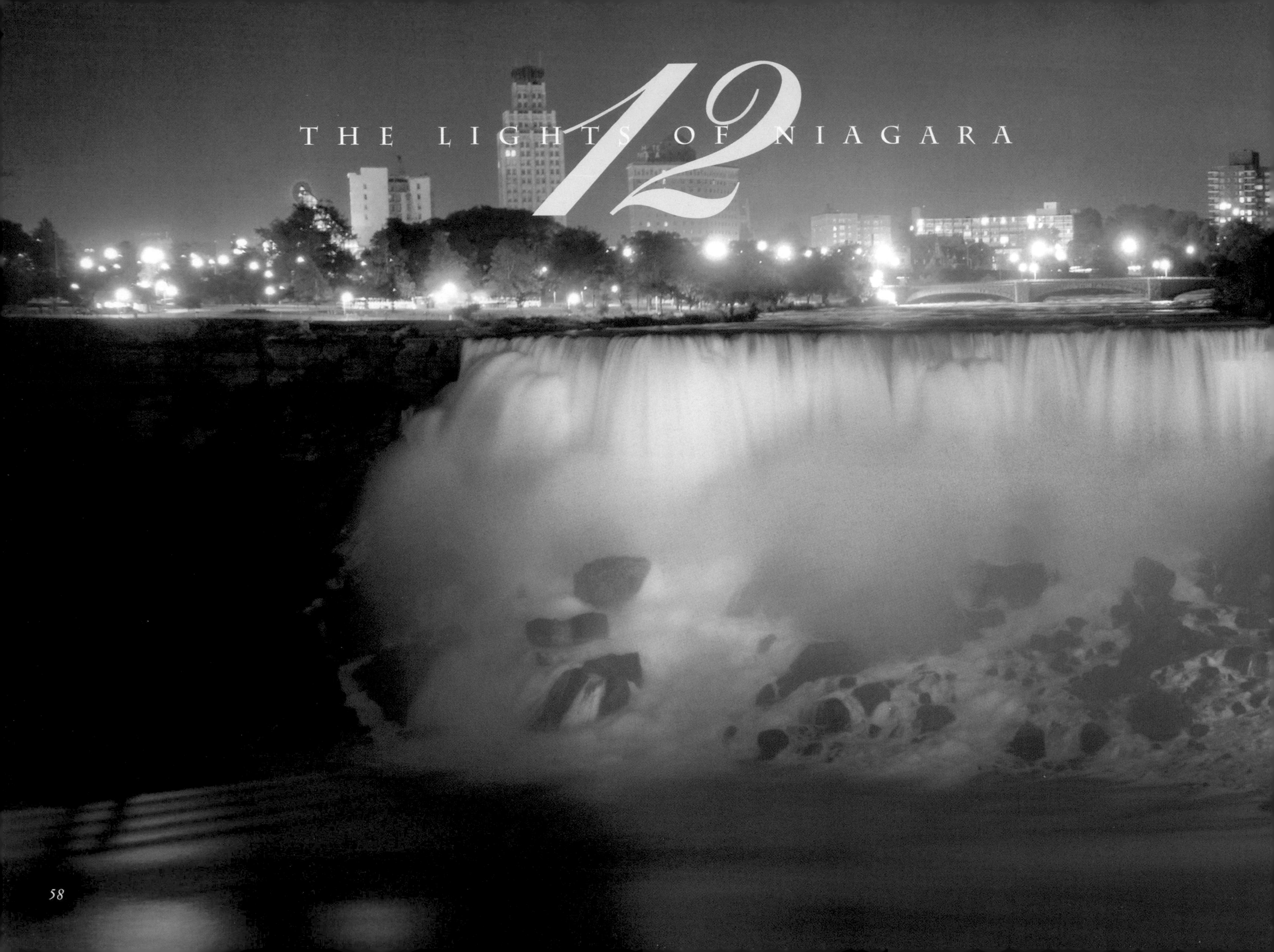

12
THE LIGHTS OF NIAGARA

The Winter Festival of Lights, started in the early 1980s, takes place from late November to early January in both Niagara Falls, New York and Niagara Falls, Ontario.

In addition to the nightly illumination of the Falls, thousands of lights and displays are located in each of these sister cities. Winter, once a relatively quiet time of the year, has now been transformed into a wonderland of lights and exciting events.

Niagara Falls

Photograph Bridal View Falls.

In the mid-twentieth century, the majority of visitors came from within a six-hour drive of Niagara Falls. Although these people still visit, Niagara Falls now receives visitors from all over the world as a result of improved air travel. Annually, approximately 12 to 14 million people visit Niagara Falls, Canada.

To have seen enough of Niagara Falls seems impossible. The longer you stay, the more you are impressed; the more you discover, the more reluctant you are to leave. In addition to the many attractions offered by the Niagara Parks Commission, there are countless other attractions to keep people of all ages amused.

Clifton Hill is still exciting, packed with wax museums, fast food outlets, gift shops and motels. At night, Clifton Hill offers a particularly great show with its flashing neon signage.

The wineries are quickly becoming a growing attraction. Some of the best Canadian wines are produced in the Niagara area and many wineries offer samples of their product and tours of their facilities. The rich soil of the area below the Niagara escarpment is perfect for growing not only grapes, but apples, peaches and pears. Visitors can pick their own basket of fruit or purchase fresh picked fruit from a roadside stand.

The nearby Niagara-on-the-Lake, the first capital of Upper Canada in 1791, is a delightful town to visit. It is also the home of the acclaimed theatrical Shaw Festival.

Want to ride a barrel over Niagara Falls? Then visit Ride Niagara where you can take a simulated trip over the Falls. There is also plenty to keep history buffs occupied, and horticulturalists and nature lovers alike will enjoy the gardens of the Niagara Parks Commission.

Wintertime has become a particularly popular time to visit with the annual Winter Festival of Lights lasting from mid November to early January.

For honeymooners, the local Niagara Falls, Canada Visitor and Convention Bureau will issue a special certificate signed by the Mayor proclaiming they visited Niagara Falls on their honeymoon. And the nightly illumination of the Falls provides lots of colourful dreams. Before leaving, be sure to take one last look at the mighty falls as the waters rush over the brink and crash down to the river below, making a mad dash to Lake Ontario, the St. Lawrence River and the Atlantic Ocean beyond. The magic of Niagara will last a lifetime.

Photographs (Left) *An aerial view of the Canadian Horseshoe Falls. (Above) Dusk on Clifton Hill.*

The Niagara River and Falls

The Niagara River is about 58 km (36 mi.) in length and is the natural outlet from Lake Erie to Lake Ontario flowing south to north.

The elevation differential between the two lakes is about 99 m (326 ft.), half occurring at the Falls themselves.

The total area drained by the Niagara River is approximately 684,000 square km (264,000 square mi.).

The average fall from Lake Erie to the beginning of the upper Niagara Rapids is only 2.7 m (9 ft.).

The Canadian Horseshoe Falls, for the most part, falls 52 m (170 ft.) into the Maid of the Mist pool.

At the American Falls, the water plunges vertically, ranging from 21 to 34 m (70 to 110 ft.) to a pile of rocks at the base of the Falls.

The Niagara Gorge extends from the Falls for 11 km (7 mi.) downstream to the foot of the escarpment at Queenston, Ontario.

The depth of the Whirlpool is 38 m (125 ft.).

Crestlines

The crestline of the Canadian Horseshoe Falls is approximately 670 m (2,200 ft.).

The crestline of the American Falls (edge to edge) is approximately 260 m (850 ft.).

The crestline of the Bridal Veil Falls is approximately 15 m (50 ft.).

The crestline of Luna Island is approximately 30.5 m (100 ft.).

Combined Volume of Flow

April 1 to Sept. 15 8:00 a.m. to 10:00 p.m.
Sept. 16 to Oct. 31 8:00 a.m. to 8:00 p.m.
2832 m3/sec (100,000 cfs) or 37.4 million Canadian Imperial Gallons per minute or 750,000 U.S.A. Gallons per second.
All other dates and times:
1416 m3/sec (50,000 cfs) or 375,000 U.S.A. Gallons per second

Note: Not all of the water goes over the Falls. The total average flow is approximately 6,000 m3/second or 212,000 cubic feet/second. The remainder of the river flow is removed upstream from the Falls and is shared equally for hydroelectric generation by Canada and the United States. The total generating capacity at Niagara is about 4 million kilowatts (5 million horsepower)

USA Gallons

6,000 m3/s = 1,590,000/second

95,400,000/minute

5,724,000,000/hour

137,376,000,000/day

Note: The U.S.A. standard is 3.8 litres and the Imperial standard is 4.5 litres.

More than 168,000 cubic m (6 million cubic ft.) of water go over the crestline every minute during peak daytime tourist hours. Or in other words ... a million bathtubs of water goes over the Falls every second!